# THE BUDDHIST WORLD

## Anne Bancroft

**MACDONALD**

**Editor**
Peter Harrison
**Managing Editor**
Belinda Hollyer
**Design**
Sally Boothroyd
**Picture Research**
Caroline Mitchell
**Production**
Rosemary Bishop

We are grateful for the assistance of
Professor J. C. Wright, London University.

First published in Great Britain in 1984
by Macdonald & Company (Publishers) Ltd
London and Sydney
A member of BPCC plc

ISBN 0 356 07524 9

Made and printed by
Henri Proost, Belgium

**Cover picture:** A group of women take
offerings of flowers and robes to one of the
great temples in Thailand.

**Endpapers:** Tibetan refugees celebrate the
third day of Losar, their New Year festival.

**Title page:** Novices before the richly
decorated wooden buildings of a Bhutanese
monastery.

**Contents page:** A member of a procession
strikes a note of gold against the vivid blue
sky of Ladakh, a small country in north-
west India on the borders of Tibet and
Kashmir.

Bancroft, Anne
    The Buddhist world.—(Religions of the
    world)
    1. Buddhism—Juvenile literature
    I. Title        II. Series
    294.3        BQ4032

    ISBN 0-356-07524-9

# Contents

# Who are the Buddhists?

**Right:** Here two Burmese women pour water over an image of the Buddha. This is one way of paying respect to the person of the Buddha himself.

**Below:** The Buddha gained enlightenment at Bodh Gaya, in north-east India. From this central point, Buddhism spread in the directions shown on the map. Today the number of Buddhists is estimated at over 500 million people.

Buddhism began with a man. He was an Indian prince called Siddhartha Gotama and he lived nearly 2500 years ago. He was a famous teacher and many people listened to him and practised what he taught. Gotama preached against war and against class, helping people whether they were rich or poor. He made peace between quarrelling landowners and helped those who were unhappy, or suffering in their minds.

## Look and listen

Gotama did not rely on miracles or gods or anything out of the ordinary. Instead he taught people to look at the results of their thoughts and actions. He showed them that if they acted wisely and well they would live happier lives. Men and women who continue to follow Gotama's teaching and example call themselves Buddhists.

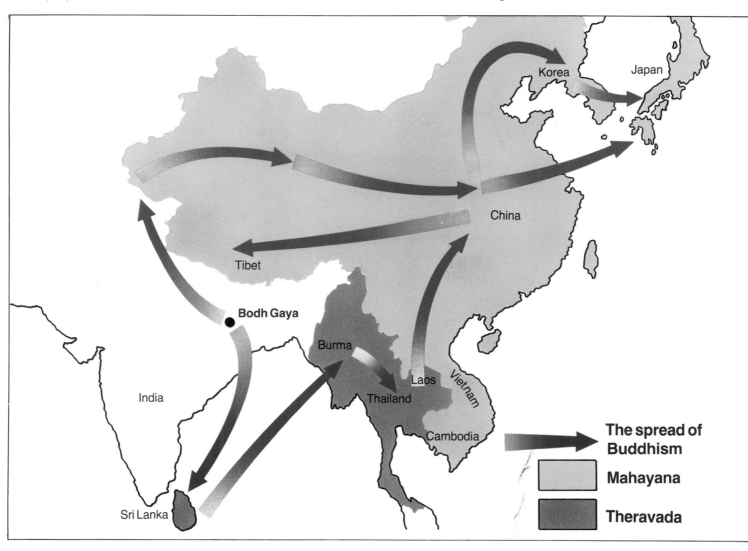

Korea

Japan

China

Tibet

Bodh Gaya

Burma

Laos

Vietnam

Thailand

India

Cambodia

Sri Lanka

**The spread of Buddhism**

**Mahayana**

**Theravada**

## The name of Buddha

The word Buddha is a title meaning 'The Awakened One'. It comes from its root *budh* which means both to wake up and to know. While people think they are awake, the Buddha believed that they spend much of their time dreaming. People may sometimes, perhaps, only think about life instead of actually living it.

Buddha also means 'The Enlightened One': a person who has understood the truth about life and so is able to help humanity. Buddhists believe that there have been other people like Siddhartha in history and that there will be more Buddhas to come.

## The spread of Buddhism

By the time the Buddha died, thousands of people in India had become his followers. During the next centuries his teaching spread throughout most of Asia. It mingled with the traditional beliefs of many countries, bringing new understanding to old beliefs. Today there are well over 500 million Buddhists in such countries as India, Nepal, China, Japan, Korea, Tibet, Cambodia, Laos, Vietnam, Malaysia, Burma, Thailand and Sri Lanka.

## East and West

Buddhism is becoming popular in the West, perhaps because it is a peaceful religion and does not ask people to believe in anything without finding out for themselves if it is true. Buddhist teachings began to be translated into European languages at the beginning of this century. As time went on, monks and nuns and teachers from as far away as Tibet and Japan came to live in the West. Now there are many Buddhist centres, and thousands of people in Europe and America practise the Buddha's teaching.

## A religion without God

Buddhism is sometimes called a religion without a God, and so hardly a religion at all. But although Buddhists do not believe in God as a divine Being, they are very conscious of a reality behind all appearances. They call it Emptiness or the Void, because it is the essence of all things but has no form of its own. The Buddha said: "There is an uncreated, timeless and formless. Were there not, there would be no help for the created."

## The human mind

Because Buddhism has no God, it also does not have an authoritarian 'Word of God', which must be accepted. Instead it believes that the human mind is a creative centre, and that this mind has a limitless capacity to change and grow, with experience.

**Above:** Large open-air gatherings honouring the Buddha play an important part in the lives of many Tibetan Buddhists.

# The life of the Buddha

Many legends surround the Buddha's birth. It is said that the earth was flooded with light and the blind were able to see; the lame walked and prisoners were freed from their chains.

The historical facts are that the baby, Siddhartha Gotama, was born 2500 years ago. He was the son of King Sudhodana, the ruler of a small kingdom in north-east India, near the present-day country of Nepal. The people he ruled were known as the Shakyas.

## The prophecy

Legend tells us that King Sudhodana asked fortune tellers to prophesy what the future would hold for his new son. All agreed that if Gotama stayed in the world he would become a great emperor, ruler of all India; but if he left the world for a holy life, he would become not an emperor but a world saviour. The king wanted his son to be an emperor and so gave him all he could desire to keep him happy.

**Below:** The tree under which the Buddha became enlightened is known as the Bodhi tree. They are grown in every Buddhist holy place. Here one fans out its branches behind a temple in Sri Lanka.

## The four signs

When Gotama was a young man he married his cousin and in time they had a baby son. Gotama should have been the happiest man on earth. But although he loved his wife and son, he was bored with the life of the palace. The beautiful clothes he wore and the fine horses he rode meant nothing to him. He wanted to find out the meaning of life and he did not know where to look.

## Seeing the signs

Legends relate how the fortune tellers warned the king not to let Gotama see an old man, a sick man or a dead man. So the king had ordered that the old, sick and dead should not be allowed near the prince.

Although the king did everything he could to prevent Gotama from seeing the old, sick or dead, an old man was overlooked one day. When Gotama went out in his chariot he saw the hobbling old man and questioned his charioteer. "Old age comes to all of us," was the reply. The next day they saw a man, pale and ill, sitting by the roadside; and on the third day they saw a dead body, with the family weeping by it. Gotama was greatly disturbed by what he had seen. He wondered why such suffering should come to people. Then, on the fourth day he saw a man with a shaven head and yellow robe, who looked serene and wise. This was an ascetic, the charioteer told Gotama—someone who had no home and sheltered in caves, begging enough food for one meal a day. The ascetic tried to live a pure life and understand the reason for existence. "I too shall live like this," thought Gotama.

## Gotama's search

That night Gotama left the palace secretly and rode to the edge of the forest. With him came the charioteer, who cut off Gotama's long hair. Then Gotama set off alone into the forest. He went to famous teachers but they did not have the answer to human suffering. Some wandering ascetics told him he should starve and then he would see the truth. So he ate very little—one grain of rice a day, it is said—but he simply became weak and ill. A milkmaid gave him food and after eating it he felt so much better that he vowed never to starve again. He would take the middle way, neither too little nor too much.

**Below:** While living as an ascetic, the Buddha starved himself until he almost became a skeleton. This sculpture shows him in that state.

# The Buddha's teaching

**Right:** The lotus flower is often used as an image in Buddhist thought. It is seen as resembling humans in their search for knowledge, because its roots are in the mud whilst its face turns toward the sun.

Gotama parted from the ascetics and went on his way. It was now six years since he had left the palace. He came to a big tree and decided to sit beneath it in meditation. He would not get up until he had become fully enlightened and found out the truth of why people suffer.

Gotama sat all night, going deeper and deeper into meditation. When the morning star shone out he suddenly saw the whole truth of existence. He was enlightened and awake. Legends describe how Mara, the evil one, hurled thunderbolts at him which turned into flowers as they reached him. At last Mara taunted him: "Nobody will understand you." Gotama touched the ground. "The earth will bear me witness," he replied. Mara was conquered.

## Deciding to teach

Because he was now enlightened, people called Gotama the Buddha. He was 35 years old. For the rest of his life, until he died at the age of 80, he walked all over the land of India. He taught ways of living which helped people to cure their suffering. He founded the Sangha, the order of monks and nuns who spent their lives spreading the teaching.

When he was dying, his followers wept and wondered what they would do. He said: "Hold fast to the truth as to a lamp. Strive to become fully awake."

## The teaching

The Buddha began to teach at Varanasi, the holy city of the Hindus. He gave his first talk in a deer park at Sarnath, on the edge of the city. It was called 'Setting in Motion the Wheel of the Law'. This was an important speech, because in it he explained the basis of all Buddhist understanding and practice.

## The wheel of the law

The Buddha drew a wheel on the ground. Then he talked about how existence is like a never-ending circle. People move round from birth through life to death, and then back to birth again. Wanting to stay on the wheel is what keeps people on it, the Buddha said. It seemed very simple. He likened himself to a doctor who tells his patient first that he is ill; second, the reason for his illness; third, that the illness can be cured; and fourth, how to set about curing it.

## The four noble truths

• In this world of time and space no-one ever experiences total satisfaction, the Buddha said. Nothing lasts. Even the happiest moments vanish.

• People suffer, he explained, because they want to keep things. They crave and grasp them and are never satisfied. They become greedy and self-centred. Greed and hatred divide nations and bring war.

• It is possible to see why people fight to keep things. Such feelings can be recognised and rooted out.

• This rooting out can be done by following new ways of thinking, speaking and acting. Whole attitudes to life can be changed and a new consciousness and outlook gained by following a simple and reasonable eightfold path.

## The eight ways to clarity

• *Understanding :* People should see clearly what they are doing with life.

• *Thinking :* They should learn to free themselves from the grip of day-dreams so that thoughts can be more clear.

• *Speech :* Talking can be used to say good things and to understand others.

• *Action :* Good acts arise when there is no clinging to the results of actions.

• *Work :* People should try not to take jobs which will harm other living creatures.

• *Effort :* They should try to use their will to cut through difficulties.

• *Mindfulness :* People should pay full attention to what they are doing.

• *Concentration :* They should try to concentrate on becoming one with the situation, whatever it is.

**Above :** This Indian painting shows the Buddha teaching in the countryside surrounded by his followers. Lotus flowers can be seen in the lake behind them.

**Far left :** The Buddha's teaching is also known as the Wheel of the Law. In this sculpture the Buddha's hands are shown in the position known as 'Turning the Wheel' (see p. 38).

# Living in the world

Everyday life, for a Buddhist, does not mean storing up a lot of money or power. It means seeing that the world is full of living creatures and organisms and that they must always be protected and helped. The Buddha said: "You should cease to do evil, learn to do good, and clarify your mind."

No-one finds it easy to clarify and control their mind and Buddhists have found that they need methods and exercises to help them. The best way, which many practise, is to learn to pay attention to what is actually seen or heard or felt without letting any past memories or future plans get in the way.

This means, for instance, looking at a tree with total attention—so that the tree itself is attended to and not the person's ideas or feelings about it.

Seeing a thing just as it is presented, without comparing it to anything else or wanting to change it, can bring an entirely new understanding of it.

## The five promises

There are no rules in Buddhism; no 'musts' or 'must nots'. But Buddhists understand that everything they do has its own result, so they try to make sensible choices. They believe that a bad action will not only affect

the person who does it but also many other people. So they try to make their actions fit properly into the situation.

To help them remember to act well, they can make five promises, called precepts:

- Not to harm any living thing.
- Not to take what is not given.
- Not to live in an over-excited way.
- Not to say unkind things.
- Not to take drugs or drink which will cloud the mind.

Because they do not like killing, most Buddhists are vegetarians. They believe that people should live in a balanced harmony with all of nature.

## The helping *bodhisattva*

In early Buddhism it was said that somebody very wise and kind, who no longer thought about themselves at all but was only concerned with the good of others, was called a *bodhisattva* (*bodhi* means wise and *sattva* means being). They would not leave the world at death but would come back again and again to save all beings, even to the last blades of grass.

Buddhists try to live up to the *bodhisattva*'s qualities—generosity, loving kindness, self-sacrifice, compassion—as they go through each day. This helps them to live in the world.

In Tibet the *bodhisattva* came to be shown in paintings as a god-like figure called Avalokiteshvara. Tibetans today pray to Avalokiteshvara, seeing him as the spirit of the Buddha. His strength is given the name of a second god, Manjushri; and Manjushri holds a flaming sword of knowledge.

## The Wheel of Life

This ever-turning wheel shows Tibetan beliefs about life. In the hub of the wheel are three creatures: a cock for greed, a snake for hatred and a pig for delusion—these, the Tibetans believe, are the forces which keep us tied to life. There are six segments in the wheel. These are worlds showing the states of mind people can go through. Moving clockwise, first there are the gods, good people who are given all they want; then the anti-gods who are jealous of those people and always at war with them.

Then there are the ghosts, looking for more. They are usually shown with mouths much too small to take in food. Then come the sad people in hell, who are suffering great mental pain. In the fifth section are pairs of animals peacefully moving about: these are people who have not developed their minds and live only for their bodies. The last section shows ordinary intelligent human beings. The Compassionate Buddha appears in each of these segments to show that whatever state of mind people are in there is always help for them.

**Above:** Yama, the Lord of the Underworld, holds the Wheel of Life. Inside the Wheel are all the states into which all living things can be reborn many times.

# Leaving the world

Shortly after the Buddha's death, his followers divided into two different groups. These were called the two great Schools— the Theravada School and the Mahayana School. The Theravadins believed that a person is an individual on their own; if they want to become awakened like the Buddha, they can. But it will be all their own work and they must rely on wisdom to carry them through to awakenment.

The Mahayanans said almost the opposite; that a person's life is linked to all others so that any of their actions will affect the whole world; that a person need not rely only on themselves but can look for help from something beyond themselves; and that love is greater than wisdom.

The countries of southern Buddhism, such as Sri Lanka, Thailand and Burma, took up Theravada. And the countries of northern Buddhism, such as Tibet, China, Korea and Japan adopted Mahayana Buddhism.

In spite of their differences, Buddhists everywhere get on well together and do not fight among themselves. What they hold in common is more than what keeps them apart. But they do have different ideas about what happens after death.

## Southern Buddhism

The Theravadins do not believe that a particular person will be reborn. But they do believe that the energies of good and bad which were created in their lifetime will be attached to a new person at birth. The energies will affect the new person's life.

**Above:** This monk is having his head shaved to purify himself in preparation for a funeral.

**Right:** When the Buddha died, he lay on his side. This image of the *parinirvana*, or Buddha entering the final state of *nirvana*, is in a temple in Rangoon, in Burma.

## Ceremonies for the dead

Theravadins follow the Hindu custom of burning the body at death. The Buddha's body was cremated and this set the example for many Buddhists, even in the West. When someone is dying in a Burmese home, monks come to comfort them. They chant verses to them, such as:

"Even the gorgeous royal chariots wear out; and indeed this body too wears out. But the teaching of goodness does not age; and so Goodness makes that known to the good ones."

After death, while the dead person is being prepared for the funeral fire, the monks continue to chant in order to help the dead one's good energies to be released from their fading personality.

The monks come with the family to the funeral. The family and all their friends give food and candles to the monks. Goodwill is created by these gifts and it is believed that the goodwill helps the lingering spirit of the dead person.

## Other worlds

In Tibet, a Mahayana country, the day of death is thought of as highly important. It is believed that as soon as the death of the body has taken place, the personality goes into a state of trance for four days. During this time the person does not know they are dead. This period is called the First Bardo and during it the person can be reached by *lamas* (monks) saying special verses to them.

It is believed that towards the end of this time the dead person will see a brilliant light. If the radiance of the Clear Light does not terrify them, and they can welcome it, then the person will not be reborn. But most flee from the Light, which then fades.

The person then becomes conscious that death has occurred. At this point the Second Bardo begins. The person sees all that they have ever done or thought passing in front of them. While they watch they feel they have a body; but when they realise this is not so, they long to possess one again. Then comes the Third Bardo, which is the state of seeking another birth. All previous thoughts and actions direct the person to choose new parents, who will give them their next body.

## Dying is easy

In Japan a form of Mahayana Buddhism called Zen is practised. Japanese Zen masters sometimes know when they are going to die.

Once master Hofaku called his monks together and said: "This last week my energy has been draining—no cause for worry. It is just that death is near."
A monk asked: "You are about to die! What does it mean? We will go on living. And what does *that* mean?"
"They are both the way of things," the master replied.
"But how can I understand two such different states?"
Hofaku answered: "When it rains it pours," and then he calmly died.

**Below:** Here, the Amida Buddha sits in the Western Paradise to which his followers believe they will go at death. His name means light and spiritual growth.

# Special days

**Right:** Pouring oil on to lamps at Vesak is a way of showing faith in what the Buddha said.

Buddhist festivals are always joyful occasions. Every May, on the night of the full moon, Buddhists all over the world celebrate the birth, enlightenment and death of the Buddha such a long time ago.

## Vesak

In Thai villages people get ready during the day. They clean their houses and hang up garlands of flowers. The men take clean sand from the river bank and spread it over the temple courtyard, where everyone walks with bare feet. Statues of the Buddha are brought out of the temple to be washed and polished and all the books come out to be dusted. When it is dark, the villagers gather with candles or small oil lamps. The biggest Buddha statue is put on a platform outside the temple and lights shine all round it. Scented water is thrown onto it. Holding their lights, everyone starts to move round the Buddha statue so that in the end it is encircled with light. This festival is known as Vesak. In the West it is called Buddha Day. It is a very happy occasion.

## The festival of the Tooth

Kandy is a beautiful city in Sri Lanka. It is built round the edge of a lake. On a small hill is a great temple which was built specially to house a relic of the Buddha—his tooth. The tooth can never be seen, it is kept deep inside many caskets. But once a year in August, on the night of the full moon, there is a special procession for it.

First of all to come are the elephants. They wear brilliant gold headdresses covered with silver studs and coloured glass to look like jewels. The biggest elephant carries a pagoda and in it rests the casket with the tooth. There is great excitement among all the watching crowds when it is seen. The tooth is carried at slow elephant pace right round the city. Some elephants wear bright cloths on their backs, others are painted all over. Each has its *mahmout* (driver) also dressed up. Following them come dancers and fire swallowers. Then another row of elephants (there are many in Sri Lanka). Fireworks go up and the festival, which is called the *peharera*, continues all night.

**Far right:** The Festival of the Tooth goes on for nine consecutive nights. More than 130 richly decorated elephants take part in the processions.

# Making offerings

**Right:** The way in which these Buddhists raise their hands is a typical gesture of devotion. This shrine is in Sri Lanka.

**Below:** As a prayer wheel turns, Buddhists believe the sacred words inside are repeated hundreds of times and released into the world.

As Buddhism is a religion without a God, it might be asked who do Buddhists pray to? Or do they pray at all?

The answer is that most Buddhists pray, but they are praying to the Buddha within themselves. They believe that the enlightened nature of the Buddha is their own real nature which they have not yet been able to reach. So when they pray, it is to that deepest part of themselves.

In Sri Lanka and Thailand the temples are always open, and many people go in during the day. They bring flowers for the Buddha statue or light a candle to show their love and respect. Usually they bow to show their gratitude for the Buddha's teaching. Then perhaps they will sit for a little time in prayer. Sometimes they put rice in front of the Buddha or light an incense stick. These are also ways of honouring the Buddha.

## The jewel in the lotus

In Tibet prayer is going on most of the time. Tibetans pray in a special way. They believe that when certain sounds and words, called *mantras*, are said many times they arouse good vibrations within the person. If a *mantra* is repeated often enough it can open up the mind to a consciousness which is beyond words and thoughts.

*Om*, as in Hinduism, is the greatest sound. It is said on its own or it is linked to three other words—'*Om mani padme hum*'—which means 'the jewel in the lotus' or 'the truth in the heart of the teaching'. '*Om mani padme hum*' is repeated everywhere. People say it as they walk down the road, monks intone it to the accompaniment of great trumpets; shopkeepers mutter it in between serving customers.

This prayer is also inscribed on revolving bronze cylinders, called prayer wheels. Every temple has a set of prayer wheels which people spin round so that the vibration is sent in all directions. All temples have it written on banners for the wind to carry to the world, and it is written on rocks on the hillsides.

Another way a Tibetan prays is by putting the hands together and then bringing them down in a continuous movement until the forehead touches the ground.

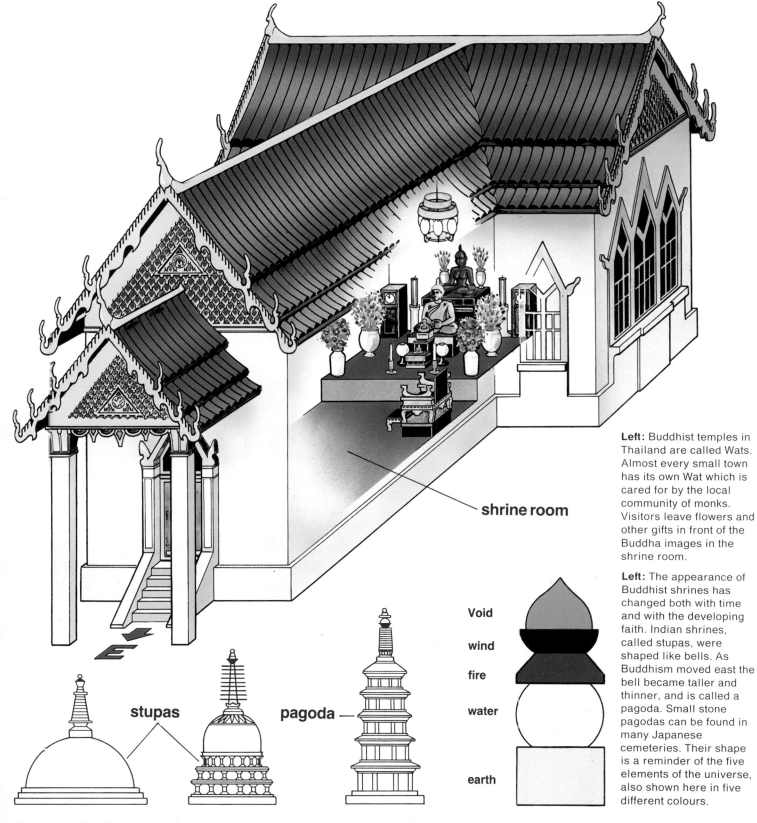

**shrine room**

**stupas**

**pagoda**

Void

wind

fire

water

earth

**Left:** Buddhist temples in Thailand are called Wats. Almost every small town has its own Wat which is cared for by the local community of monks. Visitors leave flowers and other gifts in front of the Buddha images in the shrine room.

**Left:** The appearance of Buddhist shrines has changed both with time and with the developing faith. Indian shrines, called stupas, were shaped like bells. As Buddhism moved east the bell became taller and thinner, and is called a pagoda. Small stone pagodas can be found in many Japanese cemeteries. Their shape is a reminder of the five elements of the universe, also shown here in five different colours.

## The pure land

In Japan millions of Buddhists pray to Amida Buddha, the Buddha of Infinite Light. They believe that Amida has created a Pure Land in the west and that those who have faith and repeat Amida's name in prayer will go there. Yet they also believe that Amida is really within them. An old lady of the Pure Land faith was walking along the road when she met a Zen master.

The master said to her:
"On your way to the Pure Land, eh, Granny?" She nodded.
"Holy Amida's there, waiting for you, I expect?"
She shook her head.
"Not there? The Buddha's not in his Pure Land? Where is he then?"
She rapped twice over her heart and went away. That was where the Buddha was.

# Meditation

Meditation, in Buddhism, is a way of helping the mind to settle down into a tranquil state of clarity and openness. Usually people's heads are full of buzzing thoughts. It is as though a commentator was inside them, and saying 'that's good' or 'that's awful'. The practice of meditation is a way of losing the commentator and becoming quiet and calm. Then whatever is in the world can be seen more clearly, without 'good' or 'bad', but just as it is.

The Buddha said: "In the seeing there should be just the seeing, in the hearing just the hearing, and in the thinking just the thought."

So in meditation Buddhists try to do just one thing properly. They will sit and feel their breath as it comes in and goes out. Sitting, they will become aware of their body as well as of their surroundings—of the wind and the rain. Thoughts may float across their mind but they simply let them go, always asking: "Who is the person who is listening?" In this way they hope to find their true self, find freedom from fear, and find happiness. This probably will not happen all at once; practice is important.

## The riddle of the bell

In Zen, meditation is practised in some unusual ways. For instance, a master will ask a question, or riddle, called a *koan*, such as: "Stop the sound of the distant bell"—but no bell is ringing! To try and stop a bell which is not ringing is absurd. And yet pupils must say something or they will not be able to go on with the teaching. They will meditate on it day and night until suddenly it will come to them: if I am the bell then I can stop the sound. So they say "Bong!" to the master and that is correct. They have learned to be something other than themselves (a bell). In Zen this act of identifying with another object or person is very important because that is how a *bodhisattva* helps all beings— by feeling what it is like to become them.

## Time and place

Zen also believes in identifying with any situation. If, for instance, someone wants to catch a bus but it goes off without them, they can identify with the wait for the next bus, finding the special reality of that waiting time. Or they can look at what is around them. This is also thought of as meditation.

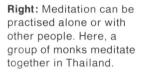

**Right:** Meditation can be practised alone or with other people. Here, a group of monks meditate together in Thailand.

## Seeing a goddess

Tibetans, too, identify with things when they meditate, but not with everyday objects in the world. They prefer to concentrate on elaborate pictures, called *tankas*. *Tankas* show the wisdom, strength, compassion and peace of the Buddha in the form of gods and goddesses. For instance, Tibetans will try to visualise (see in the mind's eye) a goddess called Tara, who stands for the Buddha's compassion. They will visualise Tara sitting on top of their head, then coming into their head, and then into their heart. They then feel that she has become them, and has given them her own quality of compassion. They have become one with Tara, they feel.

## Meditation on the mandala

As well as *tankas*, Tibetans also paint *mandalas* for meditation. A *mandala* is a design within a circle. Sometimes it is a picture with figures, such as the Wheel of Life, or it may be a series of eye-catching interwoven shapes intended to help focus thoughts. More often it is a square within a circle; this symbolises the earth. It is not meant to be flat but should always be seen as three-dimensional. It is full of colour and each colour represents a quality of the Buddha. White is for his purity, blue for the vastness of his teaching and its truth, and red is for the warmth of his nature. The colours bring the qualities to mind.

**Above:** *Mandalas* are often very complex pictures, full of small details. A meditator would try to concentrate on these, and to see them with their eyes closed.

23

# A time to learn

**Right:** This Burmese boy's father carries the begging bowl and fan which his son will use while a novice in the monastery.

**Far right top:** A novice monk is not always serious! This boy lives in a monastery in Bhutan.

**Far right bottom:** Buddhist monks and nuns have always played a large part in the education of children. Here a young Tibetan boy practises writing.

24

In many Buddhist countries, young boys of about 11 will spend some months in a monastery (communities where Buddhist monks or nuns live together). This is to give them a special education, both in ordinary subjects and in the Buddha's teaching. When they are older they can return as apprentices to learn the crafts of carpentry, wood carving and making Buddha images. Many nuns and monks are teachers in ordinary schools as well.

In Burma, the boys who will be going into the monastery are given a special feast to which the monks are invited. They are then dressed up as princes in bright silk cloth to look like Gotama before he left the palace. Mounted on white horses they ride in a colourful procession to the monastery. There, their heads are shaved and they put on yellow robes. The monastery is not a strict place but more like a village centre, so they see their parents often. They even play football, like ordinary boys, in the monastery courtyard.

## Taking the bodhisattva vow

Boys in Tibet who reach the age of 11 can go into a monastery to live as monks for the rest of their lives. One of the first ceremonies is to promise to try to become a *bodhisattva*. This means taking four vows:

- The beings of the world are numberless; I vow to save them all.
- The delusions of the world are infinite; I vow to end them all.
- The gates of the teaching are many; I vow to enter them all.
- Enlightenment is supreme; I vow to attain it.

After this the boys will spend years in hard study and meditation practice, as do all Tibetan monks and nuns. They must learn to meditate, eventually for hours at a time. They must be able to understand and recite many of the Buddha's teachings. When they are about 15, they will start having contests to see who understands most. They will spend hours debating and trying to score points over the others. They will take part in many processions and festivals as well, and learn how to make music with trumpets and how to chant scriptures.

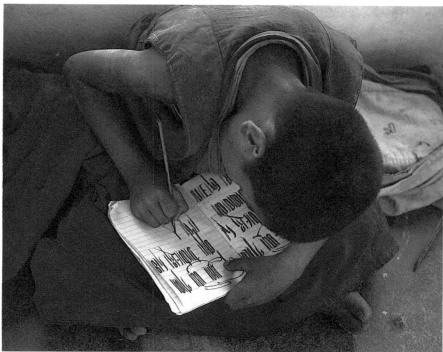

# Joining together

**Above:** These Tibetan monks, watched by their elders, are discussing points of the Buddha's teaching together.

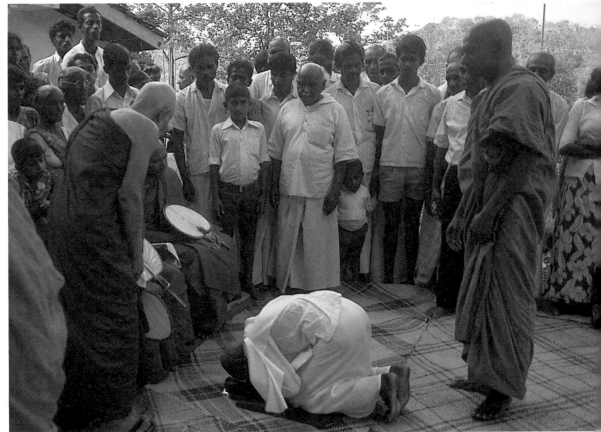

**Right:** Watched by his fellow villagers, this young Sri Lankan bows before the monks whose community he is asking to join. He wears the white robes of a novice.

26

In Sri Lanka, Thailand and Burma a monastery, as well as being a community of monks or nuns, is also a centre for the lives of those who are not monks and nuns. Visitors stay there, especially during a big festival, because hotels are scarce. Country boys live at city monasteries while they are at school or college. Families meet each other to chat in the monastery courtyard while their children play games. And as well the monastery acts as a bank, where people leave their precious things, and where valuable old books and objects are stored.

## Among people

As well as meditating, the monks do many jobs. In Sri Lanka they teach the villagers how to build schools, look after the crops and dig for wells. They also teach them how to read and write. In Thailand the monks go out every morning with empty bowls to the villagers, who heap rice, bananas and vegetables into them. This is for the monks' one meal of the day, which they must eat before noon. Many festivals take place in the courtyard of the monastery as well.

## Sitting in the snow

To be a Zen monk or nun is not easy. In the past a person might have to wait outside the monastery for days, never leaving their post, before the master would give them an interview. There is a famous story of a would-be monk who sat in the snow for many days and at last cut off his arm to show how sincere he was. Nowadays a letter from another temple is sufficient, as well as travelling clothes. These are a robe, a bamboo hat, a pair of straw sandals and cotton leggings (monks and nuns make many pilgrimages). But when the person arrives at the gate of the monastery they will still be refused entry, sometimes being pushed out.

They will then seat themselves calmly, legs crossed, and go into meditation. When night comes they knock again and this time are allowed inside. But there is no comfortable bed for them. Instead, they must sit on a cushion and meditate all night. In the morning they bow and leave again, to sit outside all day, head on their bundle. This treatment is their first lesson in humility before being admitted to the community.

**Left:** Lines of monks with begging bowls are a common sight in towns and villages in the Far East. Here a Thai woman fills the bowls of three monks with food.

# Women speaking

**Right:** Tara is a female *bodhisattva* honoured in Tibet. She is also known as Goddess of the Seven Eyes, because she has an eye in the palm of each hand, the sole of each foot, and in the centre of her forehead.

In Mahayana countries women have always practised Buddhism equally with men, whether they were nuns or villagers. Today there are many women teachers. Here is what Maureen Freedgood says. She is a *roshi*, the same status as a Zen master. "Sitting on this cushion we practise opening to the wholeness of our being; all of it. Not just our pleasant thoughts, not just our calm, lovely mind, whenever that appears, but our anger, our hurt, our fears—everything. When we accept and have compassion for that in ourselves, for every single bit of it in us—out of that comes acceptance and compassion for others. This allows us to be fearless and open to all beings—not just humans but to animals, gardens, houses, everything."

### Inside and outside

Barbara Rhodes, a Zen teacher says: "To nurture ourselves and to nurture our families means first getting to know who we are, what we are. That can come about through sitting practice, but also through opening up to the teachers that are here, whether they be Zen masters or an old man in a pickup truck." Ane-la Pema Choden is a Tibetan nun. She says: "What's important is how I handle my own path, how I work in each moment with my own mind." Both people and a person's thoughts are helpful.

### Connected with each other

A nun in a Theravada country has less status than a monk. Although the Buddha thought that men and women were equal and could both become enlightened, since that time monks have not allowed nuns equal status. But now Buddhist women want to be given more education and equality. Throughout Theravada history there have been women teachers who were not nuns. One today is Joanna Macey. She says: "In our western tradition we have been taught and conditioned to revere the individual. We take the person so seriously. It's very beautiful what the West has done in taking seriously its individual existence. Now we can take those gains and merge them with a fresh discovery of our deep interconnectedness. And honour the individuality of each whether they're halfway round the planet or not even born yet."

Aachen Naeb is a Thai teacher. She likes people to listen with open minds, not fixed on their own ideas. This is because: ". . . we must try to find out if what is being spoken is leading to the truth."

**Below:** In this women's temple in Singapore, the 'wooden fish' in the foreground is struck to produce sounds when praying or meditating.

**Left:** This busy woman pauses for a moment to light incense-sticks in a Bangkok temple.

# Tibetan Buddhism

**Right:** Every year in Ladakh monks wearing masks and costumes perform dances based on Buddhist tales. Hundreds of people come to watch.

Tibet is a country dominated by the vast Himalayan mountains. Tibetans farm in the fertile valleys. Or they are nomads, grazing herds of yaks on the plateaus and living in tents. There are no cities and the biggest town, Lhasa, is almost entirely one huge monastery. Smaller monasteries are everywhere—by the roadside or cut into the rocks or perched by a mountain stream.

Tibetans are a hardy, independent people who took Buddhism as their religion (it came from India 1500 years ago) and made of it not only a way of spiritual understanding but also a form of government. They believe that the noblest and most spiritual person should be their ruler, whom they call the Dalai Lama.

In 1950 the Chinese invaded Tibet. They believed that Tibet was part of China anyway. But Tibetans did not agree and many rebelled. Many, including the Dalai Lama, fled from Tibet. Most settled just over the border, in northern India. But others came to the West. According to a Tibetan prophecy, a time would come when they would go out and teach the "pink-faced people". That time appears to be now.

Tibet, more than any other Buddhist country, believes that all creatures are reborn from life to life. Most remain animals—it is hard to become a human. If lucky enough to be born human, a person should make the very best of their life.

### The baby born to be ruler

Tibetans believe that the Dalai Lama is like a power-point through which the forces of compassion radiate to the people. The power itself comes from the god Avalokiteshvara, who is the spirit of compassion. So it is believed that when a Dalai Lama dies, Avalokiteshvara (who is also the Buddha) simply takes on a new body and is reborn again. But which body? Finding the new Dalai Lama is a difficult process. It will be a baby and it could be from any family, rich or poor. Usually the dying Dalai Lama will have left some instructions about where to look. So *lamas* (monks) will go to that part of the country and start examining babies to see if they can find the right one. The baby should show that it recognises at least four of the previous Dalai Lama's belongings, and there are other tests. As well as the Dalai Lama, up to 200 other spiritual people, men and women, are thought to pass from life to life in this way. They are given the special name of *tulkus*.

**Below:** This *lama*'s room is filled with small *tankas* (like the one on his left), and other ritual objects. He is holding a bell in one hand. This is rung during ceremonies.

## Finding the tulku

One such *tulku* is Chogyam Trungpa. He tells of the way the *lamas* discovered him through a vision: "The vision came to a high leader called the Karmapa. The Karmapa said: 'The tenth Trungpa has been reborn in a village five days journey northwards from here. Its name sounds like two words, Ge and De; there is a family with two children; the door of the family's dwelling faces south; they own a big red dog; the son, who is nearly a year old, is Trungpa Tulku.' Three *lamas* set off immediately.

## The baby's welcome

After five days journey they reached the village of Geje. In one tent they found a baby boy who had a sister and, as the Karmapa had said, the entrance faced south and there was a red dog. As soon as the baby saw them in the distance he waved his little hand and broke into smiles as they came in. So the *lamas* felt this must be the child and gave him the gifts which the Karmapa had

sent: the sacred protective cord and the traditional white scarf. The baby took the scarf and hung it round one lama's neck in the proper way, as if he had already been taught what was the right thing to do. Delighted, the lamas picked me up, for I was the baby, and I tried to talk. The news was sent to the Karmapa, who was sure that I was the eleventh Trungpa Tulku."

## Life in the monastery

Trungpa and his mother went to live in a house near the monastery and he was taken to it every day. A few months later, when he was barely two, he was enthroned in front of an audience of 13,000 *lamas* from all parts of Eastern Tibet. When he was five, his mother left him at the monastery and returned to their village. His life from then on was one of hard study. He had one special *lama* who looked after him and was like a parent. In 1959 Trungpa came to Britain. He soon learned English and now lives in America where he teaches Tibetan Buddhism.

**Above:** The height of the crests on these monks' headdresses represents how much they have learned through studying the holy books of Buddhism. They are blowing trumpets called *shawms* which are over 2 metres in length.

# Written knowledge

**Right:** The courtyard of this monastery is filled with new books of sacred texts. The long, thin shape of the books recalls the fact that the Buddha's words were first written down on palm leaves.

Two sets of scriptures came into existence after the Buddha's death. They both evolved from his teachings, which were carried on by word of mouth for some 500 years until writing took over. One—Theravada scriptures—were compiled by the Sri Lankans in an Indian language called Pali, while the other—Mahayana scriptures—were written in Sanskrit, the classical language of India. Many of the earliest Mahayana scriptures were destroyed or lost when the Muslims invaded India, whereas the Theravada scriptures remained intact. The ideas of the lost Mahayana scriptures were carried on, however, in the writings of Tibetan and Chinese scholars, so that now a vast literature of scriptural texts and commentary from both schools exists.

## The three baskets

The Pali teachings were called the Tipitaka, the three baskets of the Law. The first basket was made up of rules for monks and nuns; the second was the actual teaching of the Buddha; and the third was a commentary on the teaching. The second is what most people read, since it contains interesting accounts of what the Buddha said and did. Here is one account:

Angoulimala was a fierce robber. He killed people as well as robbing them and everyone feared him. One day the Buddha came walking through his country. He knew about Angoulimala and was not afraid when he saw the killer was following him. "Stand still!" ordered Angoulimala. "I am still," said the Buddha (but he went on walking),

"it is you who is moving," he said. "I am not moving, I am still. It is you who is moving," shouted back Angoulimala. The Buddha turned round. "My legs move but my mind is still," he said. "Your legs are still, but your mind moves all the time with anger, hatred and feverish desire." Angoulimala saw the truth of this, was cured of his badness, and became a disciple of the Buddha.

## Believing in Mind

One of the famous Mahayana scriptures is a long poem by a Chinese, Seng-ts'an, who lived almost 1300 years ago. It is about being able to keep the mind at peace, and see clearly. Here is part of it:

*The Great Way is not difficult*
*For those who have no preferences.*
*When love and hate are both absent*
*Everything becomes clear and undisguised.*
*Make the smallest distinction, however,*
*And heaven and earth are set infinitely apart.*
*If you wish to see the truth*
*Then hold no opinions for or against anything.*
*To set up what you like against what you dislike*
*Is the disease of the mind.*
*When the deep meaning of things is not understood*
*The mind's essential peace is disturbed to no avail.*
*The Way is perfect like vast space;*
*It lacks nothing and nothing is in excess.*

दितीये त्वागते यामे सोऽद्वितीयपराक्रमः ।
दिव्यं लेभे परं चक्षुः सर्वचक्षुष्मतां वरः ॥ ७ ॥

ततस्तेन स दिव्येन परिशुद्धेन चक्षुषा ।
ददर्श निखिलं लोकमादर्श इव निर्मले ॥ ८ ॥

सत्त्वानां पश्यतस्तस्य निकृष्टोत्कृष्टकर्मणाम् ।
प्रच्युतिं चोपपत्तिं च ववृधे करुणात्मता ॥ ९ ॥

इमे दुष्कृतकर्माणः प्राणिनो यान्ति दुर्गतिम् ।
इमेऽन्ये शुभकर्माणः प्रतिष्ठन्ते त्रिपिष्टपे ॥ १० ॥

*Towards the middle of the night he whose energy and insight were unequalled
achieved the supreme vision.*

*With that pure vision he then saw the world as though in a perfect mirror.*

*His compassion became greater as he watched all creatures being born and
reborn according to their good or evil actions.*

*Those living beings whose acts are sinful pass to the sphere of misery.
Those who act well win a place in heaven.*

**Left:** These verses are
in Sanskrit, the ancient
written language of India.
They are taken from a
poem called the
*Buddhacarita*, a retelling
of the Buddha's life. This
was composed almost
two thousand years ago
by the poet Ashvaghosa.
Here, he describes the
Buddha's enlightenment.

Phandanan capalan cittan,
dūrakkhan, dhunnivārajan
ujun karoti medhāvī, usukaro va
tejanan.

*As the arrow-maker whittles
And makes straight his arrows,
So the master directs
His straying thoughts.*

Varijo va thale khitto, okamokata
ubbhato pariphandati'dan cittan
Māradheyyan pahātave.

*Like a fish out of water,
Stranded on the shore,
Thoughts thrash and quiver.
For how can they shake off desire?*

Dunniggahassa lahuno
yatthakāmanipātino cittassa
damatho sādhu, cittan dantan
sukhâvahan.

*They tremble, they are unsteady,
They wander at their will.
It is good to control them,
And to master them brings happiness.*

Sududdasan sunipunan,
yatthakamanipatinanan cittan
rakkhetha medhavi, cittan guttan
sukhavahan.

*But how subtle they are,
How elusive!
The task is to quieten them,
And by ruling them to find happiness.*

**Left:** These verses are
taken from the
*Dhammapada*, a
collection of the Buddha's
sayings which is part of
the Pali Tipitaka.

# Visiting holy places

**Right:** Here, pilgrims can be seen at Adam's Peak. Some are already starting their long climb up the mountain, also known as Siripada.

Pilgrimages are popular in Buddhist countries. Since India was the scene of the Buddha's life, many pilgrims come from other countries to visit the important places. One, Lumbini Grove near Kapelavastu in Nepal, is where he was born. Here the great Buddhist King Ashoka set up a stone pillar in honour of the event. Another place, where the Buddha was enlightened, was some distance away from Lumbini, at Bodh Gaya. A descendant of the famous Bodhi Tree under which he was enlightened grows here and a temple tower stands beside it. A stone beneath the tree is marked with a footprint, which is said to be the Buddha's, and the tree itself is often bedecked with colourful prayer flags.

Another important place, Sarnath, is now a suburb of the city of Varanasi, and because it is easy to get to it is probably the most popular of all. Here the Buddha preached his first sermon in a deer park. The deer park still exists and there is also a large *stupa* (monument) built by King Ashoka in the park.

## Sri Lankan treasures

As Sri Lanka has been a Buddhist country for over 2000 years it has many places of pilgrimage. One of the most beautiful is Adam's Peak, a high mountain overlooking the sea. Long flights of steps wind up and up. At the top is a rock with what is said to be the Buddha's footprint on it marking the place where the Buddha stepped ashore on his third visit to the island—although no-one is sure that he ever went to Sri Lanka.

The other well known places are Anaradhapura and Polonnaruwa where great monasteries and shrines once stood, and where huge Buddhas are carved out of rock. They are a very impressive sight, and one pilgrim wrote this about them: "I am able to approach the Buddhas barefoot and undisturbed, my feet in wet grass, wet sand. Then the silence of the extraordinary faces. The great smiles. Huge and yet subtle. Filled with every possibility, questioning nothing, knowing everything, rejecting nothing . . . I was suddenly jerked clean out of the habitual half-tied vision of things and an inner clearness, clarity, as if exploding from the rocks themselves, became evident and obvious."

## Born in a lotus

Tibetans make pilgrimages joyful occasions with music and dancing. There are many places of pilgrimage on the borders of Tibet, in northern India. One is the Dalai Lama's palace. Another is the lake from which Padmasambhava, the founder of Tibetan Buddhism, is said to have emerged as a baby —born in a lotus blossom. He is greatly revered by Tibetans, and when he took the teachings of the Buddha to Tibet many flocked to hear him. He demanded bags of gold dust. The bags were brought, filled with gold dust which had been collected over centuries. Padmasambhava opened them out and the wind carried all the gold away. Then he said: "The teachings are more important." It is believed that the lake of Padmasambhava is the bluest in the world, and the source of healing powers.

**Below:** These pilgrims are dancing in a field in Sarnath, near the site of the Buddha's first sermon.

# 'Flowers are visions'

Zen is a Japanese way of Buddhism which began in China. It is considered the most direct way to enlightenment. There is a verse which describes Zen clearly:

*A special understanding outside the scriptures,*
*No dependence on words and letters,*
*Direct pointing to the heart of man,*
*Seeing into one's own nature.*

So Zen is self-reliant and does not advise living by anything other than a person's own authority. A Zen master, who is teacher and guide, is not the supreme authority and even the Buddha is not. "If you come across the Buddha in your path, kill him," a Zen master said. He meant that no ideas about the Buddha, however wonderful and wise, should come between a person and his own direct experience of truth. This makes Zen a deeply spiritual path. It also tells people how to go about living in the world:

*When walking just walk,*
*When sitting just sit,*
*Above all, don't wobble!*

**Above:** Sand and moss gardens like this one have been made in Japan to express the tranquil spirit of Zen. The meaning of the gardens lies in their simplicity.

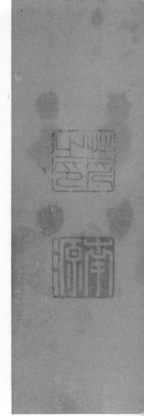

**Right:** These men are practising karate in a Tokyo park. Karate is a form of self-defence which grew out of the Zen masters' teaching of self-awareness.

36

## Seeing the world anew

There are two stages for the follower of Zen. The first is to reach the point where resistance in them lets go, and suddenly they see the world anew, all barriers dropped. This moment is called *satori*, meaning sudden illumination, and there are many descriptions of it. Han-shan says: "I took a walk. Suddenly I stood still, filled with the realisation that I had no body or mind. All I could see was one great illuminating Whole —perfect, lucid and serene. I felt as clear and transparent as though my body-mind did not exist at all."

The second stage is to enter the world again in order to live for the benefit of all others, animals as well as humans. Having had such an experience of illumination, people will not want things for themselves but instead will be able to give to the needs of others.

## The ways to illumination

As well as sitting in meditation, Zen has devised other ways of freeing the mind. One is through story. Zen literature is full of dialogues between masters and pupils which all point the way to understanding. Here is one:

A monk said to a master: "I still become easily upset. I long to have peace of mind. Will you help me?"

"My, what an interesting condition," said the master, "Bring out your mind then and I'll help you."

"But it's impossible to bring out one's mind," protested the monk.

"Why, then, I've already given you peace of mind," replied the master.

## Poetry

Similar to story is *haiku*, a form of poetry in short verses. Here is one:

On a bare branch
A rook roosts:
Autumn dusk

## The martial arts

When Buddhism came to Japan 800 years ago, the *samurai* (the warrior class) saw it as a life and death struggle with one's own nature. The martial arts of judo, karate and others grew up with this idea.

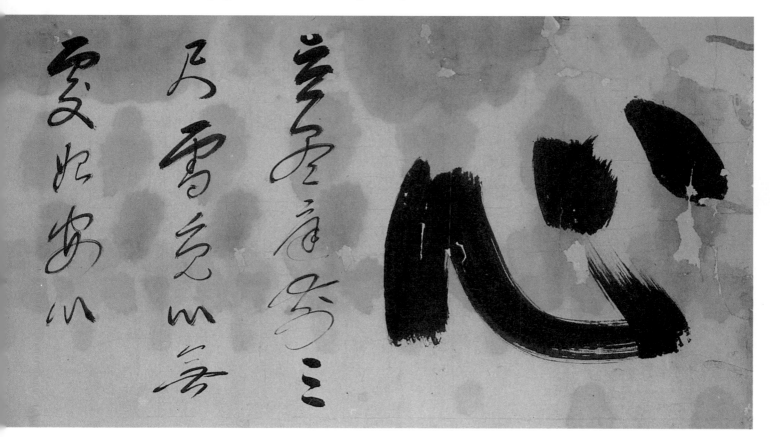

**Below:** Brush and ink handwriting, such as this example, is one of the exercises practised by Zen monks.

# Buddhist art

**Far right:** This girl is renewing the gold leaf on a statue of the reclining Buddha. This statue is 46 metres long.

In the Mahayana countries, paintings came to include many versions of the Buddha. As a *bodhisattva*, he dominated art in Tibet and was often shown surrounded by minor gods such as the Guardians of the Four Directions, Serpent Kings, Yama the King of Death, angry demons and animal spirits such as the hare in the moon.

Tibetans and Nepalese use bright colours in their paintings because they believe colours symbolise different parts of the mind. Shape is also used to help the mind reach enlightenment, especially the round shape of the *mandala* with its inner structure. Statues too are important, because they convey attitudes of mind in their gestures, especially the hands.

## The golden Buddhas

As Buddhism spread south, north and east from India along the great trade routes, it inspired art wherever it went. Temples were gilded and decorated to a high degree, their walls covered with painted scenes from the Buddha's life. Statues were painted with gold leaf. In Bangkok today coloured glass is used to give brilliant effects on temple roofs. At the Temple of the Emerald Buddha in Bangkok, £6,000,000 has just been spent on renovations, one third of which is for gold alone.

Buddhist art in India and Sri Lanka can be seen in early cave paintings and rock carvings. The cave paintings in Ajanta in India are among the finest in the world.

**Right:** A group of boy monks learn to make a *mandala*. This design will be used in a festival and then destroyed. The following year, it will be made again.

**Right:** The gestures of the hands and fingers in Buddhist art can have special meaning. They are called *mudras*. The first *mudra* 'A' is called 'Turning the Wheel of the Law'. In the second, 'B', one hand is raised in a gesture of protection, while the other hand grants a wish.

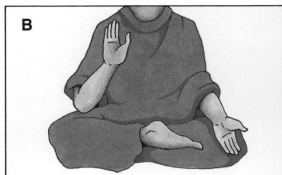

## Paintings about the Buddha

Buddhist artists have always loved to paint scenes from the Buddha's life. They have often added delightful imaginary details. For example, when painting Siddharta leaving the palace, they sometimes add flying angels which hold up the hooves of his horse so that they make no sound, and no-one hears him leaving.

There is a very popular legend which many Buddhist artists have painted. The Buddha's cousin tried to kill him by turning a wild elephant loose on the path where the Buddha was walking. The animal charged, but as it came close it felt the power of the Buddha's compassionate love for all creatures. The power was so great that the elephant stopped, knelt down, and paid honour to the Buddha.

## Great space

In China, Buddhist art reached a high state of perfection in the Sung Dynasty (935–1279 AD) and China, Korea and Japan have remained true to that tradition ever since. Closest to the feeling of it is a style of painting called *sumie-e* which uses black ink diluted with water which is then brushed on to paper or silk. Just a few strokes will show, for instance, a waterfall and rocks, or a poem written in bold calligraphy (handwriting). A Zen master's writing would show the standard of his insight. Space was seen as the basis for all Zen art— objects exist in space, words come out of air, the feeling of *satori* is that of infinite space. And into backgrounds of lake, sky, rock and tree, the Zen masters were painted as very human—scowling, shouting or laughing, catching fish. As well, gardens came to be made in the same way—space, with just a few rocks and trees and sometimes sand.

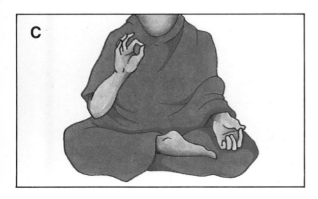

**Left:** In 'D', the hands are 'calling the earth to witness'. When the Buddha became enlightened he touched the earth. In 'C', the hands are in the gesture of teaching.

# Buddhism in the West

The 'come and see for yourself' attitude of Buddhism attracts many Westerners. They are not asked to believe in anything, but to follow the Buddha's advice of testing ideas first. With the growth of easy travel and communication, the West has been able to find out more about Buddhism in this century than in all the time before. The informality and emphasis on practice of Buddhism appeals to many Westerners.

## The influence of Buddhism
Buddhist attitudes of peace, mindfulness and care for all living creatures have come to be the concerns of many groups in the West. Buddhists believe that all things should be looked after: the earth, plants, birds, insects and animals. This is close to the feeling among many people in recent years that the human race should stop polluting the atmosphere and destroying the surface of the earth by cutting down forests.

**Below:** Here, a whole group of Buddhist priests attend a ceremony for Vietnamese refugees in California.

## Buddhism travels West
Although the Buddha's teachings have been known in countries throughout the Far East for over 1500 years, very few people in

Europe or America would have known what the word 'Buddhist' meant unless they had been born in the last 50 years.

Over a century ago people from France, the Netherlands, Great Britain, and other European countries began to travel to the Far East. Many of them returned with Eastern ideas, and so Europeans began to hear about Buddhism.

More recently, Buddhist people have moved to the West. Many of them have been refugees from conflict. Many Tibetans, for example, fled from their country after the Chinese takeover in 1959. The wars in Indo-China in the 1950s and 1960s led many Vietnamese people to move to and settle in Europe and America. Other Buddhists from countries such as Thailand have established businesses in the larger Western cities. They have all brought their Buddhist beliefs to their new homes, and helped to set up Buddhist centres.

## At a Buddhist Centre
The basis of Buddhist practice in the West, as in the East, is meditation, and people may sit on cushions with their legs folded and

their hands in their laps. They will practise breathing or meditative walking.

At other times they will listen to a talk. They will also do some chanting, and make offerings to the Buddha image in its shrine. A Theravadin group will be very quiet and peaceful. They may form themselves into lines to give food to the monks in the morning and expect to hear a talk during the day. A Tibetan group can be more active, chanting, asking questions and ringing bells.

A Korean Zen group will walk around and bang whatever is handy as loudly as possible. They will also spend much time chanting. Japanese Zen groups are more restrained and spend a lot of time in meditation.

**Here to stay?**
The activities at Buddhist centres allow people to find different ways of understanding Buddhism. Perhaps this will mean that still more Westerners will become Buddhists.

**Left:** A procession of monks and nuns celebrate the opening of a pagoda in the town of Milton Keynes in Great Britain.

# Further information

## A glossary of useful words

**Ashoka** an Indian king who lived in the 3rd century BC. He became a Buddhist and spread Buddhism throughout India and Sri Lanka.

**Avalokiteshvara** the essence of the Buddha's wisdom and compassion given the name and form of a god.

**Bardo** the intermediate state between death and rebirth according to Tibetan Buddhism.

**bikkhu** a Theravadin monk. These monks can be recognised by their yellow robes and shaven heads.

**Bodhi** enlightened wisdom. The name given to the tree under which Siddhartha became a Buddha.

**bodhisattva** often called the Buddha of Compassion. One who remains in the world in order to help all others.

**Buddha** the title given to Siddhartha Gotama when he became enlightened. It means 'one who is awake'.

**Dalai Lama** the spiritual leader of Tibetan Buddhists and the exiled ruler of Tibet.

**dana** giving. Buddhists believe that giving to others is an important part of their lives.

**Dharma** truth, law or teaching. The Dharma is the teaching of the Buddha.

**dukkha** the Buddhist word for suffering.

**Hinayana** means 'little vehicle'. It was a name given by the Mahayanans to the Theravadins in early Buddhism.

**karma** a word meaning action and the results of action; the law of cause and effect.

**karuna** active compassion. Help given to any in need from a sense of wise understanding.

**koan** a problem put into apparently non-sensical language. Habits of thought need to be broken in order to understand it.

**lama** a Tibetan religious teacher and monk.

**Mahayana** one of the two main schools of Buddhism. The word means Great Vehicle.

**mandala** a design or picture inside a circle used as an aid to concentration.

**mantra** a special word or sound which is repeated as a form of meditation.

**Mara** the Evil One, who tempted the Buddha under the Bodhi Tree.

**meditation** ways of quiet composure which go beyond thought. Meditators usually sit with legs folded, but many other activities are also included in the term.

**metta** loving-kindness. An essential quality for Buddhists. The Metta Sutra is one of the most important and popular teachings.

**mudra** a gesture. Buddha images have their hands in different positions and each of these gestures has a meaning.

**nirvana** a blissful state. Mahayanans see it as the completion of life, the unfolding of the infinite possibilities of the Buddha-nature, and applaud the saint who stays in touch with life. Theravadins regard it as the final escape from life by extinguishing all longings. They honour those who choose to turn away from life.

**Padmasambhava** the Indian holy man who is said to have brought Buddhism to Tibet.

**Pali** a language of ancient western India used by the Theravadins for writing the scriptures.

**peharera** a procession in Sri Lanka.

**prajna** wisdom beyond the ordinary. *prajna* is said to arise in the mind as the student in Buddhism gains insight.

**precept** a vow. Every Buddhist tries to live by five precepts and monks and nuns should follow ten.

**puja** an act of devotion. Buddhists make offerings to images of the Buddha, usually offering flowers, lighted candles or incense.

**rebirth** a new birth, accompanied by energies from a previous life.

**roshi** a Zen master. There are also women *roshis*.

**rupa** body or form. It usually refers to an image of the Buddha.

**samsara** earthly existence.

**sangha** an assembly. In Mahayana countrie it means the whole Buddhist community. In Theravada countries it means the monastic order.

**Sanskrit** the ancient classical language of India.

**satori** a state of new consciousness. It may vary from a flash of intuitive awareness to the bliss of *nirvana*.

**Shakyamuni** a name given to Gotama meaning wise man of the Shakyas (the people of his country).

**sila** behaviour. In particular, the discipline attached to the precepts.

**skandha** the five elements of life which forr a being. In man, the five elements are: the body, feeling (emotions), perception (throug the senses), mind, and consciousness.

**sutra** the name means teaching or guide line and is used to describe the Buddhist scriptures.

**tanka** a Tibetan religious picture.

**tantra** a teaching associated with Tibet in which the use of the senses is cultivated to bring about enlightenment.

**Tathagata** a title used by the Buddha in speaking about himself, meaning—he who has come and gone as former Buddhas.

**Theravada** one of the two main schools of Buddhism. The word means 'the tradition of the elders'.

**Tipitaka** the 'three baskets' which form the Pali Canon, the scriptures of the Theravadins. A similar set exists for Mahayana Buddhists.

**upasaka** a lay disciple who keeps to the eightfold path while living in the world.

**Uposatha** the four monthly holy days which continue to be observed in Theravada countries—the new moon, full moon and quarter moon days.

**Vesak** the celebration on the night of the full moon in May which commemorates the Buddha's birth, enlightenment, and passing away.

**Zen** a Mahayana school which began in China and is now strongly alive in Japan and Korea. It is known for the dynamic immediacy of its teaching, its martial arts, flower arrangement, landscape gardening and tea ceremony. These are all thought of as forms of meditation.

# More festivals

Many Buddhists love festivals and they take place throughout the year, especially in countries like Sri Lanka, Thailand and Burma. As well as the ones described on page 18, here are some more which take place in Thailand.

### Songkran

This festival goes on for several days during the middle of April. Everyone puts on new clothes. They gather together beside the riverbank, carrying fishes in jars to put into the water, for April is so hot in Thailand that the ponds dry out and the fish would die if they were not rescued.

### The Water Festival

This takes place during Songkran. People go to the beach or river bank with jars or buckets of water and splash each other. Sometimes they sit in the river with their clothes on. When everyone is wet, there is a boat race on the river.

### Fighting Kites

Also during Songkran, a great 'male' kite called Chula is sent up and then smaller 'female' kites called pukpows try to bring him down. Many people take part with their own kites and it goes on all day.

### The Ploughing Festival

In May, when the moon is half-full, two white oxen pull a gold-painted plough, followed by four girls dressed in white who scatter rice seeds from gold and silver baskets. This is to celebrate the Buddha's first moment of enlightenment. It happened when the Buddha was seven years old. He had gone with his father to watch the ploughing. The young Buddha saw a boy eat a frog thrown up by the ploughing, which made him understand that everything passes away.

### Loy Krathong

This is another moon festival. As the moon rises people gather on the river bank, carrying cups made of leaves. Inside the cups are lighted candles. The cups are put onto the river and float away. As they go, all bad luck is supposed to disappear.

### Kathin

At the end of the rainy season there is a festival for the monks. They will be given new robes made by the villagers at a special ceremony. Even the king gives a robe.

### The Elephant Festival

The Buddha used the example of a wild elephant which, when it is caught, is harnessed to a tame one to train it. In the same way, he said, a person new to Buddhism should have the special friendship of an older Buddhist. To mark this saying, Thais holds an elephant festival on the third Saturday in November. Over 200 elephants are brought to show how strong they are, and how gentle at the same time.

The Sanskrit text on p.33 is reproduced from E. H. Johnson's parallel text of the *Buddhacarita*, Baptist Mission Press, Calcutta, 1936. The translation is adapted from the English in the same source.

The Pali text is from T. W. Rhys Davids' text of the Dhammapada, © Pali Text Society, London, 1899–1921. The translation is © Thomas Byrom, from his Wildwood Press edition of the *Dhammapada*, London, 1976.

# Books for further reading

*Buddhist Tales for Children* Christina Albers (Buddhist Publications Society 1972)
*A Life of Buddha for Children* Christina Albers (Buddhist Publication Society 1974)
*Our Buddhist Friends* Joan Alcott (National Christian Education Council 1978)
*Festivals of the Buddha* Anne Bancroft (Religious and Moral Education Press 1984)
*Zen: Direct Pointing to Reality* Anne Bancroft (Thames and Hudson 1981)
*Buddhists and Buddhism* Martha Patrick (Wayland Publishers 1982)
*What the Buddha Taught* Walpole Rahula (Gordon Frazer 1972)
*Zen Flesh, Zen Bones* Paul Reps (Pelican 1977)
*The Life of the Buddha* H. Saddhatissa (Unwin Paperbacks 1976)
*The Buddha's Way* H. Saddhatissa (George Allen and Unwin 1971)
*Born in Tibet* C. Trungpa (George Allen and Unwin 1976)
*The Spirit of Zen* Alan Watts (Grove Press 1958—also in other editions)

# Places to visit

It is often a good idea to write or telephone before visiting.

Buddha Vihara, 146 Lea Road, Wolverhampton WV3 0LQ. 0902 341296. The tradition is Theravada and Indian. There is a Buddhist Sunday School for children.

The Buddhapadipa Temple, 14 Calonne Road, Wimbledon Parkside, London SW19. 01 946 1357. Thai Buddhists of the Theravada School. A fine pagoda has been built here.

London Buddhist Vihara, 5 Heathfield Gardens, London W4 4JU. 01 995 9493. This is a Sri Lankan Theravadin centre.

The Chithurst Forest Monastery, Chithurst, Petersfield, Hampshire. Midhurst 4886. A Theravadin monastery which accepts visitors. There is a small group of monks who live permanently in the monastery.

Kagyu Samye-ling Tibetan Centre, Eskdalemuir, Langholm, Dumfriesshire, Scotland. Eskdalemuir 232. A Tibetan painter of *tankas* lives at this oldest and biggest Tibetan centre.

Kampo Gangra Kagyu Ling, 1A Reynard Road, Chorlton, Manchester M21 2DB. 061 881 5221. A Tibetan centre.

Kham Tibetan House, 2 Rectory Lane, Ashdon, Nr. Saffron Walden, Essex. 0799 84 415. Lama Chime Rinpoche who runs this centre is the head of Tibetan teaching in Britain.

Lam Rim Buddhist Centre, Pentwyn Manor, Penrhos, Raglan, Gwent NP5 2 LE. 060 085 383. A residential Tibetan centre.

Milton Keynes Peace Pagoda. This was put up in 1983 and is well worth a visit. For directions apply to Milton Keynes Buddhist Group, 28 Glovers Lane, Heelands, Milton Keynes, Bucks. 0908 319256.

Throssel Hole Priory, Car Shield, Hexham, Northumberland NE47 8AJL. 049 85 204. A Zen monastery.

West Midlands Buddhist Centre, 47 Carlisle Road, Edgbaston, Birmingham B16 9BH. 021 454 6591. Two residential Theravadin *bikkhus* are here and much goes on. There is a children's magazine published.

The Zendo, 36 Victoria Parade, Ashton, Nr. Preston, Lancs. 0772 726031. This is a newly formed Zen centre.

# Helpful organisations

For a more extensive list of Buddhist groups, obtain the Buddhist Directory from the Buddhist Society at the address below.

The Buddhist Society, 58 Ecclestone Square London SW1 1PH. 01 834 5858. All schools of Buddhism are taught here.

Friends of the Western Buddhist Order, The London Buddhist Centre, 51 Roman Rd., Bethnal Green, London E2. 01 981 1225.

# Index

## Illustration credits

Key to positions of
illustrations:
(T) top, (L) left,
(B) bottom, (R) right.

### Artists

Dave Eaton: 38–39
Raymond Turvey: 8, 21

### Photographic sources

Art and Architecture
   Collection: 12B
Cam Culbert: 8, 36B
Douglas Dickins: 10, 35, 36T
Werner Forman Archive:
   28L, 37/Greta Jensen:
   endpapers, 25B, 26T, 38
Format/Anita Corbin: 28
   28R/Jenny Matthews:
   20R
Geoscience Features:
   contents page, 9, 30L
Robert Harding Picture
   Library: title page, 22, 32
Michael Holford: 13, 15, 17, 23
Alan Hutchison Library:
   cover, 11, 14T, 16T, 18, 24, 26B
Christine Osborne: 12T
Bury Peerless: 16B, 20L, 34
Richard Ravensdale: 30L, 31
Rex Features: 14, 41
UNICEF: 25T
Mireille Vautier: 38, 40
ZEFA: 19, 27, 29

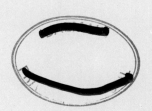